Hugo's Simplified System

Italian Verbs
Simplified

Hugo's Language Books Limited

5th impression 1990

Original edition compiled by

L. Panizza Jackson M.A.
and
dott. **A. M. Saporito Minghetti**

Set in 9/11pt Linotron 202 Times by
Tek Translation Ltd., London W12 8LH
Printed and bound in Great Britain by
Courier International Ltd, Tiptree, Essex

Preface

The greater part of this book is for reference only, and in common with others in our 'Simplified' and 'Three Months' series its object is to save the student's time by giving no rules other than those actually necessary.

The models of regular verbs (pages 14–17) should be learned first of all. When the regular verbs have been mastered, the irregular ones should present little difficulty.

No English for the subjunctive should be learned. The translation usually given—'that I may speak' or 'might speak'—is most misleading and often absolutely wrong. The only safe way is to learn when to use it.

Fuller conjugations of the compound tenses, and of the negative and interrogative forms, are omitted because they require no learning whatever. Some publications treat them exhaustively and only succeed in disheartening the student. Their formation is precisely the same throughout every verb in the language—learn one and you have learned them all.

Where necessary, we show which syllable takes the stress by placing a dot under the vowel concerned (as in pạrlano, *they speak*). This dot is, of course, not used in written Italian.

We believe that this book will be found a great help to the beginner who has not yet mastered Italian verbs, and an invaluable reference book for the more advanced student.

Contents

Structure of a verb 5

Subject pronouns 7

Italian conjugations 9

Infinitive, gerund and participle 12

Complete regular conjugations 14
'Parlare', 'temere'
'Dormire', 'capire'

Auxiliary verbs 'essere' and 'avere' 18
Complete conjugations

Formation and use of tenses 20
Present, imperfect, past definite, future, conditional,
present/imperfect subjunctive, imperative

Compound tenses 26

When to use 'essere' 28

Subject/object agreement with past participles 30

The passive voice 31

Impersonal verbs 31

Reflexive verbs 34

'Dovere' and 'potere' as auxiliaries 36

Negative and interrogative forms 38

Irregular verbs 39
Tables showing irregularities
Complete alphabetical list of irregular verbs 89

A model English verb 95

Structure of a verb

The verb is the most important part of speech in any language, and should therefore be learned as thoroughly as possible. If you are a little uncertain about its general structure, the following notes may help to refresh your memory. See also pages 95–96 for a model English verb, partially conjugated.

In this book you will find tables showing the conjugations of Italian verbs. To conjugate a verb means to show all its different forms.

Verbs can be *transitive* or *intransitive*. Transitive verbs are so called because they transmit the action from the subject to the object. Intransitive verbs convey a complete meaning without the addition of an object. *Roger hit* conveys no special meaning, but *Roger* (subject) *hit* (verb) *the car* (object) is a complete sentence. The verb *hit* is transitive. *It rains, she smiles*, make sense without the addition of an object. The verbs *rains, smiles* are intransitive.

Many verbs can be transitive or intransitive depending on their use in a particular sentence. *I'm singing* is intransitive, but *I'm singing a song* is transitive. *He grew* is intransitive, *he grew a beard*, transitive.

Verbs consist of two *voices* (active and passive), four *moods* (infinitive, indicative, subjunctive and imperative), three principal *tenses* (present, past, future), two *numbers* (singular and plural), and three *persons* in each number (1st, 2nd and 3rd).

In the active voice, the subject of the verb is the doer of the action expressed: *Susan* (subject) *is eating* (verb). The active voice often expresses a state or condition: *the river flows, the children rest.* In the passive voice, the subject receives the action expressed: *The apple was eaten, the car was hit.*

Of the four moods, the *infinitive* is the word given in the dictionary (*dimostrare*, to show; *rimanere*, to stay) and is in effect the name of the verb. It expresses the action itself, without any reference to time or to the person doing the action. In Italian, the infinitive is called an

5

indefinite mood, and is discussed together with participles and gerunds. This book will discuss infinitives, participles and gerunds together as well.

The *indicative* is by far the most used mood. It indicates or expresses a thing as a fact in present, past, or future time, rather than as a wish or a possibility.

The *subjunctive* has almost completely disappeared in English, but is still vigorous in Italian. It expresses wish or possibility (*Se fossi ricca!* If I were rich!); it is nearly always found in dependent sentences introduced by a form of *che*. For a full explanation, see our 'Italian in Three Months'.

The *imperative* mood is used for giving an order or command (*Si accomodi*, Sit down! *Va' via*, Go away!). The imperative has only one tense, the present, and only two persons, the 2nd (*you*) person singular and plural. However, expressions such as *Andiamo!* (Let's go!) and *Mangiamo!* (Let's eat!) are also classified as imperative.

If a verb has only one person or thing as its subject, its *number* is *singular*. If it has more than one person or thing as its subject, its number is *plural*. *I'm studying* is singular; *They're fighting* is plural. The 1st person is identified by the personal pronouns *I* and *we*; the 2nd person by *you* (singular and plural), and the 3rd person by *he, she, it,* and *they*. Tenses are always arranged in the following order:

1st person singular	I paint
2nd person singular	you paint
3rd person singular	he, she, it paints
1st person plural	we paint
2nd person plural	you paint
3rd person plural	they paint

Subject pronouns

Where in English personal subject pronouns such as *I, you, he, she, we, they* are necessary with verbs, in Italian they are rarely needed as the ending of the verb gives information about the person: *Compro,* I buy; *comprano,* they buy.

A useful rule for Italian is to avoid using *io, tu, lui, lei, noi, voi, loro* unless you have a particular reason for adding them, such as to avoid ambiguity or a desire for emphasis.

Ambiguity normally arises in the 3rd persons singular and plural. *Compra* can mean *he buys, she buys,* or *you buy.* In the 3rd person in Italian, you also have a wide choice of subject pronouns and the greatest difficulty in deciding upon which one to use.

In every conversation and letter-writing to friends, use *lui* and *lei* for *he* and *she. Egli* for *he* is slightly formal, and *ella* for *she* even more so, but you will come across these forms in books as well as in newspapers and magazines, and to some extent in conversation. *Essa* for *she* is also used sometimes although this form is usually reserved for an object rather than a person. Thus

> *Lui va in montagna quest' estate*
> He's going to the mountains this summer

> *Lei va al mare*
> She's going to the sea

In everyday conversation and letter-writing to friends, use *loro* for *they. Essi* and *esse* are used in more formal written Italian, or to make a distinction between a masculine *they* and a feminine *they.*

Never translate *it* when it is the subject of a verb. There do exist the forms *esso* and *essa* for the masculine and feminine *it* as subject, but the safest policy is to avoid using them:

> *La casa è vecchia e sembra anche piccola*
> The house is old and it also seems small

E'una bella giornata
It's a lovely day

In English, whether you address the Queen or a close relative, the correct form is *you*. In Italian, on the contrary, there are two forms of address, a familiar form and a polite one. With friends, relatives, colleagues, and children, use the familiar *tu* and *voi*.

N.B. Throughout this book, *tu* will always be translated by *you*, its modern equivalent. The 2nd person singular in English used to be *thou*. As this form is obsolete, it would be confusing to equate it with the Italian *tu*, which the student will find very much alive when he goes to Italy.

With acquaintances, elders and betters, *Lei* is used in the singular. In the plural, the corresponding form *Loro* often gives way nowadays to *voi*, which is also used extensively in addressing meetings or speaking to an audience.

With *tu* and *voi* the 2nd person singular and plural is used; with *Lei* and *Loro*, the 3rd person singular and plural is used. Consequently, the forms for *Lei* and *Loro* are exactly the same as those for *he, she, it*, and *they*. Italian subject pronouns will not be given in the tables that follow, but for your reference you will find below the corresponding forms in English and Italian for the various persons:

1st person singular	I	*io*
2nd person singular	you (familiar)	*tu*
3rd person singular	he, she it	*lui, lei*
	also you (polite)	*Lei*
1st person plural	we	*noi*
2nd person plural	you (familiar)	*voi*
3rd person plural	they	*loro, essi, esse*
	also you (polite)	*Loro*

Italian conjugations

There are three conjugations in Italian, recognized by the endings *-are, -ere, -ire* of the infinitive. The first conjugation is recognized by the ending *-are* as in *parlare* (to speak), *cambiare* (to change); the second conjugation by the ending *-ere* as in *credere* (to believe), *dividere* (to divide); the third by the ending *-ire* as in *dormire* (to sleep), *finire* (to finish). The part of the infinitive preceding the ending is called the stem. Italian verbs are conjugated by adding a variety of different endings to the stem, as you can see in the table of regular verbs, pp. 14–17.

The First Conjugation

All verbs of the 1st conjugation—and there are some six thousand—are regular with the exception of four very common ones: *andare* (to go), *dare* (to give), *fare* (to do or to make), and *stare* (to be, stay, remain or stand).

There are some minor spelling changes within certain groups of 1st conjugation verbs:

1. Verbs ending in *-care* and *-gare,* like *cercare* (to look for) and *pagare* (to pay), add *h* before endings beginning with *e* or *i* in the present and future tenses so as to preserve the same sound of the stem throughout. See the present and future tenses of *pagare* below:

> Present: *pago, paghi, paga, paghiamo, pagate, pagano*
> Future: *pagherò, pagherai, pagherà, pagheremo, pagherete, pagheranno*

2. Verbs ending in *-ciare* and *-giare,* like *cominciare* (to begin), and *mangiare* (to eat), drop the *i* in *-ciare* and *-giare* before endings beginning with *e* or *i* in the present and future tenses because in these circumstances the *i* is not necessary to preserve the sound of the stem. See the present and future tenses of *mangiare* that follow:

Present: *mangio, mangi, mangia, mangiamo, mangiate, mangiano*
Future: *mangerò, mangerai, mangerà, mangeremo, mangerete, mangeranno*

3. Verbs ending in *-iare* drop the *i* (before the *i* ending of the 2nd person of the present tense) if the *i* is not in the stressed syllable of the verb. Thus *studiare* becomes *studio, studi*; while *spiare* becomes *spio, spii*.

The Second Conjugation

While in the 1st conjugation there are very few irregular verbs, in the 2nd conjugation there are very few regular ones.

There are alternative forms for the past definite of some 2nd conjugation verbs. These forms will sometimes be encountered and therefore need to be recognized, but the learner will always be correct in using the regular ones, found in the table on p. 15.

You will find below the regular and alternative forms for the verb *credere* (to believe). Note that alternative forms exist only for the 1st and 3rd persons singular and the 3rd person plural.

Regular: *credei, credesti, credé, credemmo, credeste, crederono*
Alternative: **credetti**, *credesti*, **credette**, *credemmo, credeste,*
credettero

In the present tense of some 2nd conjugation verbs, the pronunciation changes while the spelling of the stem and endings remains exactly the same. Thus in verbs ending in *-cere* and *-gere*, like *vincere* (to conquer), *torcere* (to twist), *leggere* (to read), and *spingere* (to push), the pronunciation changes when *o* or *a* follow the *c* or *g*. For example, look at the following present tenses of *vincere* and *leggere*:

*vin**c**o, vinci, vince, vinciamo, vincete, vin**c**ono*
*leg**g**o, leggi, legge, leggiamo, leggete, leg**g**ono*

The Third Conjugation

Most verbs of the 3rd conjugation insert *-isc-* between the stem and the endings of the present tense of the indicative and subjunctive.

The following verbs and their compounds are conjugated like *partire* (to leave) and **never** insert *-isc-*:

aprire	to open	*partire*	to leave
avvertire	to warn	*pentirsi*	to repent
bollire	to boil	*seguire*	to follow
convertire	to convert	*servire*	to serve
coprire	to cover	*soffrire*	to suffer
cucire	to sew	*sortire*	to go out
divertire	to entertain	*venire*	to come
divertirsi	to enjoy oneself	*vestirsi*	to get dressed
fuggire	to flee	*udire*	to hear
morire	to die	*uscire*	to go out

There are a few verbs which may be conjugated with or without *-isc-*. The most common are:

mentire (to lie); *mento* or *mentisco*
inghiottire (to swallow); *inghiotto* or *inghiottisco*
applaudire (to applaud); *applaudo* or *applaudisco*

If in doubt, consult a modern Italian dictionary.

Infinitive, Gerund & Participle

The infinitive

The infinitive must often be used in Italian where in English you would have a choice between an infinitive or a gerund. The infinitive is also used where in English a gerund would have to be used as, for example, after a preposition:

*Mi piace **nuotare***
I like to swim *or* I like swimming

*Per me, il **cucinare** è un divertimento*
For me, cooking is a lot of fun

*Quest'olio si usa per **cucinare***
This oil is used for cooking

*Ci vuole pazienza nel **guidare***
One needs patience in driving

The gerund

The gerund in Italian is formed by adding *-ando* or *-endo* to the stem: *parlare—parlando, credere—credendo, dormire—dormendo*. It corresponds to the *-ing* form in English: *speaking, believing, sleeping*. The gerund in Italian is seldom used. You will come across it in the present and imperfect progressive tenses (see under heading Idiomatic Tenses) and in a few other cases. When it is used on its own as a noun it must be translated into English by a phrase or clause:

***Sbagliando** si impara*
One learns by making mistakes

***Fumando** troppo, ci si rovina la salute*
When you smoke too much, you ruin your health

The participle

The present participle in Italian, formed by adding *-ante* or *-ente* to the stem (*parlare—parlante, credere—credente, dormire—dormente*), also corresponds to the *-ing* form in English. This form, however, is not used as a verb any more but rather as an adjective or a noun as the examples below will show:

un **brillante** *successo*	a brilliant success
una commedia **divertente**	an amusing comedy
un uomo **importante**	an important man
un **commandante**	a commander
un **rappresentante**	a representative
un **combattente**	a combatant
un **insegnante**	a teacher
un **assistente**	an assistant

See also p. 30 for more concerning the past participle.

Complete regular conjugations

INFINITIVE:	**to speak parlare**	**to fear temere**
GERUND:	speaking parlando	fearing temendo
PAST PARTICIPLE:	spoken parlato	feared temuto
PRESENT INDICATIVE:	I speak, etc.	I fear, etc.
	parlo	temo
	parli	temi
	parla	teme
	parliamo	temiamo
	parlate	temete
	parlano	temono
FUTURE:	I shall speak, etc.	I shall fear, etc.
	parlerò	temerò
	parlerai	temerai
	parlerà	temerà
	parleremo	temeremo
	parlerete	temerete
	parleranno	temeranno
CONDITIONAL:	I should speak, etc.	I should fear, etc.
	parlerei	temerei
	parleresti	temeresti
	parlerebbe	temerebbe
	parleremmo	temeremmo
	parlereste	temereste
	parlerebbero	temerebbero
IMPERFECT:	I was speaking, etc.	I was fearing, etc.
	parlavo	temevo
	parlavi	temevi
	parlava	temeva
	parlavamo	temevamo
	parlavate	temevate
	parlavano	temevano

PAST DEFINITE: I spoke, etc.   I feared, etc.
                parl*ai*   tem*ei* (tem*etti*)
                parl*asti*   tem*esti*
                parl*ò*   tem*é* (tem*ette*)
                parl*ammo*   tem*emmo*
                parl*aste*   tem*este*
                parl*arono*   tem*erono* (tem*ettero*)

PRESENT SUBJUNCTIVE: (No English equivalent is possible)
                parl*i*   t*e*ma
                parl*i*   t*e*ma
                parl*i*   t*e*ma
                parl*iamo*   temi*amo*
                parl*iate*   temi*ate*
                parl*ino*   t*e*m*ano*

IMPERFECT SUBJUNCTIVE: (No English equivalent is possible)
                parl*assi*   tem*essi*
                parl*assi*   tem*essi*
                parl*asse*   tem*esse*
                parl*assimo*   tem*essimo*
                parl*aste*   tem*este*
                parl*assero*   tem*essero*

IMPERATIVE: (See page 24 for English equivalents)
Familiar: parl*a* (tu)   t*e*m*i* (tu)
                parl*iamo* (noi)   temi*amo* (noi)
                parl*ate* (voi)   tem*ete* (voi)

                parl*i* (Lei)   t*e*ma (Lei)
Polite: parl*ino* (Loro)   t*e*m*ano* (Loro)

INFINITIVE:	**to sleep dorm_ire_**	**to understand cap_ire_**
GERUND:	sleeping dorm_endo_	understanding cap_endo_
PAST PARTICIPLE:	slept dorm_ito_	understood cap_ito_
PRESENT INDICATIVE:	I sleep, etc.	I understand, etc.
	dormo	capisco
	dormi	capisci
	dorme	capisce
	dormiamo	capiamo
	dormite	capite
	dormono	capiscono
FUTURE:	I shall sleep, etc.	I shall understand, etc.
	dormirò	capirò
	dormirai	capirai
	dormirà	capirà
	dormiremo	capiremo
	dormirete	capirete
	dormiranno	capiranno
CONDITIONAL:	I should sleep, etc.	I should understand, etc.
	dormirei	capirei
	dormiresti	capiresti
	dormirebbe	capirebbe
	dormiremmo	capiremmo
	dormireste	capireste
	dormirebbero	capirebbero
IMPERFECT:	I was sleeping, etc.	I was understanding, etc.
	dormivo	capivo
	dormivi	capivi
	dormiva	capiva
	dormivamo	capivamo
	dormivate	capivate
	dormivano	capivano

PAST DEFINITE:	I slept, etc.	I understood, etc.
	dormii	capii
	dormisti	capisti
	dormì	capì
	dormimmo	capimmo
	dormiste	capiste
	dormirono	capirono

PRESENT SUBJUNCTIVE: (No English equivalent is possible)

	dorma	capisca
	dorma	capisca
	dorma	capisca
	dormiamo	capiamo
	dormiate	capiate
	dormano	capiscano

IMPERFECT SUBJUNCTIVE: (No English equivalent is possible)

	dormissi	capissi
	dormissi	capissi
	dormisse	capisse
	dormissimo	capissimo
	dormiste	capiste
	dormissero	capissero

IMPERATIVE: (See page 24 for English equivalents)

Familiar:

	dormi (tu)	capisci (tu)
	dormiamo (noi)	capiamo (noi)
	dormite (voi)	capite (voi)

Polite:

	dorma (Lei)	capisca (Lei)
	dormano (Loro)	capiscano (Loro)

Complete auxiliary conjugations

INFINITIVE:	**to be ęssere**	**to have avęre**
GERUND:	being essęndo	having avęndo
PAST PARTICIPLE:	been stąto	had avųto
PRESENT INDICATIVE:	I am, etc.	I have, etc.
	sọno	ho
	sęi	hąi
	è	ha
	siąmo	abbiąmo
	sięte	avęte
	sọno	hąnno
FUTURE:	I shall be, etc.	I shall have, etc.
	sarò	avrò
	sarąi	avrąi
	sarà	avrà
	saręmo	avręmo
	saręte	avręte
	sarąnno	avrąnno
CONDITIONAL:	I should be, etc.	I should have, etc.
	saręi	avręi
	saręsti	avręsti
	sarębbe	avrębbe
	saręmmo	avręmmo
	saręste	av węste
	sarębbero	avrębbero
IMPERFECT:	I was, etc.	I had, etc.
	ęro	avęvo
	ęri	avęvi
	ęra	avęva
	eravąmo	avevąmo
	eravąte	avevąte
	ęrano	avęvano

PAST DEFINITE:

I was, etc.	I had, etc.
fui	ębbi
fosti	avęsti
fu	ębbe
fummo	avęmmo
foste	avęste
furono	ębbero

PRESENT SUBJUNCTIVE: (No English equivalent is possible)

sia	ąbbia
sia	ąbbia
sia	ąbbia
siamo	abbiąmo
siąte	abbiąte
siano	ąbbiano

IMPERFECT SUBJUNCTIVE: (No English equivalent is possible)

fossi	avęssi
fossi	avęssi
fosse	avęsse
fossimo	avęssimo
foste	avęste
fossero	avęssero

IMPERATIVE: (See page 24 for English equivalents)

Familiar:		
	sii (tu)	ąbbi (tu)
	siamo (noi)	abbiąmo (noi)
	siąte (voi)	abbiąte (voi)
Polite:	sia (Lei)	ąbbia (Lei)
	siano (Loro)	ąbbiano (Loro)

19

Formation & use of tenses

Present

Note that the endings for the 1st person singular (*parlo, credo, dormo, finisco*), the 2nd person singular (*parli, credi, dormi, finisci*), and the 1st person plural (*parliamo, crediamo, dormiamo, finiamo*) are the same for all conjugations.

The stress for the 3rd person plural falls on the same syllable as the stress for the 1st, 2nd and 3rd persons singular as follows:

desidero	*desideri*	*desidera*	—	—	*desiderano*
abito	*abiti*	*abita*	—	—	*abitano*

A present tense verb in Italian such as *parlo* expresses the English *I speak, I am speaking, I do speak*. There is an Italian present progressive, *sto parlando*, I am speaking, but it is used far less than the English. (For its specific uses, see section on idiomatic tenses.) Avoid this tense and use the ordinary present tense unless you are quite sure of what you are saying.

In Italian there are no auxiliary verbs for asking questions or expressing negation. (See section on the negative form and the interrogative form.)

The English present perfect progressive used with expressions of time is translated into Italian by the present. Thus:

How long have you been living here?
*Da quanto tempo **abiti** qui?*

I have been living in London for two years
***Abito** a Londra da due anni*

Imperfect

This is the easiest Italian tense to form—but not the easiest to use! The endings are the same for all conjugations; the only change is in the characteristic vowel of the infinitive: *parlare—parlavo* etc., *credere—credevo* etc., *dormire—dormivo* etc., fin*ire—finivo* etc.

The imperfect tense is easily recognized by the presence of the letter *v* in all persons singular and plural for all conjugations. This letter is not used as a regular part of an ending in any other tense.

The imperfect Italian verb *parlavo* expresses the English *I was speaking, I used to speak*, as well as *I spoke*. This tense is used whenever writing descriptive passages or whenever referring to actions repeated in the past:

A thick fog covered the valley
*Una fitta nebbia **copriva** la valle*

Every year we went to the mountains
*Tutti gli anni **andavamo** in montagna*

The imperfect is always used in Italian to refer to an action that is continuing while another takes place:

While I was reading, the telephóne rang
*Mentre **leggevo**, suonò il telefono*

There is a tendency for verbs of thinking, willing, believing and feeling to use the imperfect instead of the past definite or the present perfect. Thus:

I wanted to leave
***Volevo** andar via*

I thought I'd take the tram
***Pensavo** di prendere il tram*

I had a headache. I felt ill
***Avevo** mal di testa. Mi **sentivo** male*

Past Definite

The endings of this tense are very similar in all three conjugations. In all forms but one (*parlò*), the endings are introduced by the characteristic vowel of the infinitive. The stress always falls on this characteristic vowel, never on the stem. An accent is generally used in the 3rd person singular (parlò, credé, dormì, finì).

The above holds true for regular verbs only. Unfortunately, this tense is more irregular than any other, but even so, there is a pattern formed within the irregular past definite of 2nd conjugation *-ere* verbs. The 1st and 3rd person singular and the 3rd person plural are always the irregular forms, and the other persons are always regular. This rule is very important to remember as irregular *-ere* verbs are very numerous. See below the regular and irregular forms of the past definite of *rispondere* (to answer), and *piacere* (to be pleasing):

	rispondere		*piacere*
REGULAR FORMS	IRREGULAR FORMS	REGULAR FORMS	IRREGULAR FORMS
—	risposi	—	piacqui
rispondesti	—	piacesti	—
—	rispose	—	piacque
rispondemmo	—	piacemmo	—
rispondeste	—	piaceste	—
—	risposero	—	piacquero

In Italian, this tense need hardly ever be used in conversation. In Northern Italy, in fact, Italians tend to use the present perfect instead. To express *I spoke to him*, they would say *gli ho parlato* rather than *gli parlai*. In Southern Italy, on the other hand, this tense is still used in conversation. It is certainly used in written Italian whether of a journalistic or literary bent.

Future and Conditional

For both future and conditional tenses, the entire infinitive less the final vowel is used as a stem to which endings are added. In the 1st conjugation, however, the characteristic vowel *a* changes to *e*: *abitare—abiterò, abiterei*, etc. In these two tenses, the stress always falls on the endings, never on the stem.

The 3rd person singular and plural of the conditional are easily recognized by *-bb-*:

*abitere**bb**e, abitere**bb**ero*; finire**bb**e, **finirebb**ero.

The endings of the familiar forms of the conditional are deceptively similar to the past definite; note carefully the difference between *parlasti—parlaste* of the past definite and *parleresti—parlereste* of the conditional; between *credesti—credeste* and *credesti—credereste*; *dormisti—dormiste* and *dormiresti—dormireste*.

The future and conditional are employed in Italian as in English. *Partirò domani* can be expressed in English as *I'll leave tomorrow* or *I'll be leaving tomorrow*; *Partirei domani* can be expressed *I'd leave tomorrow* or *I'd be leaving tomorrow*.

The conditional of *potere* (*potrei, potresti,* etc.) expresses the English *could*; and the conditional of *dovere* (*dovrei, dovresti,* etc.) the English *should* = *ought to*. (For more on *could* and *should,* see section on 'dovere' and 'potere' as auxiliary verbs.)

Present and Imperfect Subjunctive

For learning purposes there are only two conjugations in the present subjunctive, for the endings of the *-ere* and *-ire* verbs are alike in this tense. In the 1st conjugation, the characteristic vowel *a* changes to *i*, while in the 2nd and 3rd conjugations the characteristic *e* and *i* both change to *a*.

The imperfect subjunctive can always be recognized by -ss-: *parlassi, credessi, finissi.* Exceptions are the forms for the 2nd person plural *parlaste, credeste, finiste,* which are the same as the past definite.

For the use of the subjunctive, consult Hugo's 'Italian in Three Months.'

The Imperative

Strictly speaking, the imperative exists only for *tu* and *voi.* A *noi* form (*Mangiamo!* Let's eat! *Partiamo!* Let's leave!) is now classified with the imperative. The *tu, noi,* and *voi* forms make one pattern.

When *Lei* and *Loro* were introduced into Italian for formal address, the imperative for these was taken over from the 3rd persons of the present tense of the subjunctive, and constitute a second pattern. It is much easier to learn the two patterns separately.

The imperative for *tu, noi,* and *voi* is *exactly the same as the present tense.* There is only one exception to this rule: the *tu* form of a first conjugation verb such as *parlare* is *parla!*

The negative imperative for *tu* is *non* plus the infinitive: *Non fumare!* Don't smoke! *Non partire!* Don't leave! *Non piangere!* Don't cry!

There are a few irregular verbs with an irregular imperative for *tu:*

dare to give   *da'*
Dammi quel bicchiere! Give me that glass!

stare to be, stay   *sta'*
Sta' fermo! Keep still!

andare to go   *va'*
Va' via! Go away!

fare to do, make   *fa'*
Fa' presto! Hurry up!

dire to say, tell   *di'*
Dimmi la verità! Tell me the truth!

You have probably noticed that in all of these very common verbs, the final *i* of the 2nd person simply drops off. When pronouns are added—there are two examples above—the beginning consonant is doubled.

Essere and *avere* also have irregular imperatives for *tu* and *voi*. See the table of auxiliary verbs.

The imperative for *Lei* and *Loro,* we repeat, is exactly the same as the 3rd persons of the present subjunctive. No more need be said.

Note that in Italian the *noi* form of the imperative is often written without an exclamation point, and can easily be confused with an ordinary present tense. *Andiamo fuori* could thus mean *We are going out* or *Let's go out!* You must judge by the context.

Compound tenses

Verbs may be compounded in Italian with *avere* or *essere*. The auxiliary *avere* is compounded with *avere,* and the auxiliary *essere* with *essere.* These two are shown in the following table, together with examples of ordinary verbs that take *avere* or *essere* when compounded.

Note that the final *e* of *avere* is often dropped in the perfect infinitive: *aver mangiato, aver parlato.*

Note also that the past participles of verbs taking *essere* must agree in number and gender with the subject: *stato* and *partito* (*below) become *stata, partita* if feminine, the plural forms being *stati, partiti* (masculine), *state, partite* (feminine).

INFINITIVE PERFECT
to have had, spoken: *avere avuto, parlato*
to have been, left: *essere stato, partito*

GERUND PERFECT
having had, spoken: *avendo avuto, parlato*
having been, left: *essendo stato, partito*

PERFECT
I have had, spoken: *ho avuto, parlato*
I have been, left: *sono stato,* * *partito**

PLUPERFECT
I had had, spoken: *avevo avuto, parlato*
I had been, left: *ero stato, partito*

PAST DEFINITE PERFECT
I had had, spoken: *ebbi avuto, parlato*
I had been, left: *fui stato, partito*

FUTURE PERFECT
I shall have had, spoken: *avrò avuto, parlato*
I shall have been, left: *sarò stato, partito*

CONDITIONAL PERFECT
I should have had spoken: ***avrei*** *avuto, parlato*
I should have been, left: ***sarei*** *stato, partito*

PERFECT SUBJUNCTIVE
abbia *avuto, parlato*
sia *stato, partito*

PLUPERFECT SUBJUNCTIVE
avessi *avuto, parlato*
fossi *stato, partito*

When to use 'essere'

1 *Essere* is used with verbs indicating motion:

andare   to go
arrivare   to arrive
entrare   to enter
giungere   to arrive
raggiungere   to reach
fuggire   to flee
cadere   to fall down
partire   to leave
ripartire   to leave again
scappare   to dash, escape
tornare   to return
ritornare   to return
venire   to come
uscire   to go out

Note that *salire* (to go up) and *scendere* (to go down) take *essere* when there is no object, but *avere* when there is one.

Sono salito in autobus
I got into the bus

Ho salito le scale
I went up the stairs

2 *Essere* is also used with verbs expressing an action or activity the subject undergoes:

crescere   to grow
diventare, divenire   to become
dimagrire   to grow thin
invecchiare   to grow old
nascere   to be born
maturare   to mature

28

morire to die
ringiovanire to grow young
rimanere to remain, stay

>*Come sei cresciuto!*
>How you've grown!

>*Sono diventati ricchi*
>They've become rich

>*Lei è nata a Roma*
>She was born in Rome

3 With verbs expressing chance:

accadere to happen
avvenire to happen
capitare to happen
succedere to happen
toccare (*a*) to concern
dipendere to depend

>*Che cosa è successo?*
>What happened?

>*Ieri me è accaduto qualcosa di strano*
>Yesterday, something strange happened to me

4 With all passive reflexive verbs.

Subject/Object agreement with past participles

Verbs compounded with *essere*

The past participle agrees in gender and number with the subject.

Il treno è partito/I treni sono partiti
The train has left/The trains have left

La ragazza è uscita/Le ragazze sono uscite
The girl has gone out/The girls have gone out

Verbs compounded with *avere*

The past participle agrees with a direct object pronoun placed immediately in front of the verb, if the direct object is a third person. Study the following examples:

Abbiamo portato i pacchi ad Elena
We took the parcels to Elena's
Li abbiamo portati ad Elena
We took them to Elena's

Ho comprato una macchina da cucire
I've bought a sewing machine
L'ho comprata
I've bought it

The past participle does not agree with an indirect object, but it does agree with the pronoun *ne* (of it, of them):

Quante mele hai comprato? Ne ho comprate cinque
How many apples have you bought? I've bought five (of them)

Hanno mangiato la torta? Ne hanno mangiate due fette
Have they eaten the cake? They've eaten two slices (of it)

The passive voice

The passive voice is formed with the auxiliary *essere* (to be) and the past participle. Remember that the past participle, after *essere*, must agree in gender and number with the subject.

The verb *venire* can be used in the passive as an auxiliary instead of *essere*:

Il Manzoni viene molto lodato
Manzoni is praised a great deal

Il ladro venne arrestato dai carabinieri
The thief was arrested by the police

Impersonal verbs

Impersonal verbs have no person or thing as their subject, and are used only in the third person. Some common examples (including verbs which refer to the weather) are:

piove (from *piovere*)   it's raining
nevica (*nevicare*)   it's snowing
grandina (*grandinare*)   it's hailing
tuona (*tuonare*)   it's thundering
lampeggia (*lampeggiare*)   there's lightning
bisogna (*bisognare*), *occorre* (*occorrere*)   it is necessary
capita (*capitare*), *accade* (*accadere*), *avviene* (*avvenire*)   it happens
pare (*parere*), *sembra* (*sembrare*)   it seems
basta (*bastare*)   it is enough
conviene (*convenire*)   it is convenient

Occorre far benzina
It is necessary to get petrol

Pare che sia tornato a casa
It seems he's gone home

Reflexive verbs

Reflexive verbs can hardly be said to exist as such in English, but they are very common in Italian. The student should be very careful about translating Italian reflexive verbs by an English reflexive pronoun. Some reflexive verbs in Italian have nothing whatsoever to do with reflexive pronouns: *comportarsi*, to behave; *lamentarsi*, to complain; *sentirsi*, to feel. Other reflexive verbs might possibly be translated by a reflexive pronoun in English, but would be better translated another way:

lavarsi   to get washed (*rather than* to wash oneself)
vestirsi   to get dressed (*rather than* to dress oneself)

Reflexive pronouns in Italian are used to express a reciprocal action:

Ci scrivevamo ogni giorno
We used to write to each other daily

I giocatori si lanciavano la palla
The players threw the ball to each other

All other compound tenses of reflexive verbs take *essere*, and the past participle agrees in gender and number with the subject.

Example of a reflexive verb

INFINITIVE: *to enjoy onself* divertirsi

GERUND: *enjoying oneself* divertendosi

PRESENT INDICATIVE: *I enjoy myself, etc.*
mi diverto
ti diverti
si diverte
ci divertiamo
vi divertite
si divertono

FUTURE: *I shall enjoy myself* mi divertirò

CONDITIONAL: *I should enjoy myself* mi divertirẹi

IMPERFECT: *I was enjoying myself* mi divertịvo

PAST DEFINITE: *I enjoyed myself* mi divertịi

PRESENT SUBJUNCTIVE: mi divẹrta

IMPERFECT SUBJUNCTIVE: mi divertịssi

IMPERATIVE:
enjoy yourself divẹrtiti (*fam.*)
let us enjoy ourselves divertiạmoci (*fam.*)
enjoy yourselves divertịtevi (*fam.*)

enjoy yourself si divẹrta (*polite*)
enjoy yourselves si divẹrtano (*polite*)

PRESENT PERFECT: *I have enjoyed myself*
mi sono divertịto (*fem.*: divertita)
ti sei divertịto (*fem.*: divertita)
si è divertịto (*fem.*: divertita)
ci siamo divertịti (*fem.*: divertite)
vi siete divertịti (*fem.*: divertite)
si sono divertịti (*fem.*: divertite)

Idiomatic tenses

'Stare' + gerund

This construction is used in the present and imperfect, and sometimes in the future, to emphasize that a particular action is being done
at a particular moment of the present, past or future. It also draws
attention to the continuity of the action referred to. Although its
translation corresponds to the English progressive, it is not used
nearly as frequently.

> *Che fai in questo momento?*
> *Non vedi,* **sto scrivendo** *una cartolina*
> What are you doing right now?
> Can't you see, I'm writing a postcard

> *Quando Carlo tornò,* **stavo preparando** *la cena*
> When Charles came back, I was preparing the supper

'Stare per' + infinitive

> **Sto per** *partire*
> I am about to leave *or* I am just leaving

> **Stavo per** *accendere la luce*
> I was about to turn on the light *or* I was just turning on the light

'Andare a' + infinitive

> **Vado a** *fare la spesa*
> I am going to do the shopping

> **Andavo a** *prenotare i biglietti*
> I was going to book the tickets

'Avere' + 'da' + infinitive

This means *to have to*, and can be used instead of *dovere*:

> *Abbiamo da fare le valigie*
> We have to pack our suitcases

> *Ho da dirti qualcosa*
> I have to tell you something

'Andare' + past participle

This means *must be* + past participle; it can also be used instead of *dovere*:

> *Questa carne va fritta presto*
> This meat must be fried quickly

> *Questo va fatto subito*
> This must be done immediately

'Fare' + infinitive

Use this when you want to convey the meaning *to have something done*:

> *Faccio lavare il pavimento*
> I'm having the floor washed

> *Ha fatto fare tanti vestiti*
> She's had so many dresses made

> *Faranno pulire tutta la casa*
> They'll have the whole house cleaned

'Dovere' & 'potere' as auxiliaries

Both *dovere* and *potere* often have many ways of being translated into English, and it is even more difficult to translate the many English forms of *must* and *can* into Italian.

Dovere

1 This verb can mean 'to have to', 'must', 'to be obliged to', 'to be supposed to'. For example:

Devo scrivergli
I must write to him/I have to write to him/I'm supposed to write to him

Dovevo partire alle sei
I had to leave at six/I was supposed to leave at six

Dovrò partire la settimana prossima
I'll have to leave next week/I'll be obliged to leave next week

2 *Dovere* can also mean 'ought to' or 'should', when it is always translated by the conditional and conditional perfect:

Dovrei andare a trovarlo
I ought to go and see him/I should go and see him

Dovrebbero vendere quella casa
They ought to sell that house/They should sell that house

Sarei dovuto andare via
I ought to have gone away/I should have gone away

Avrebbero dovuto venderlo
They ought to have sold it/They should have sold it

3 *Dovere* meaning 'must be', 'must have been' (present and imperfect plus essere):

Devono essere molto ricchi
They must be very rich

Sua sorella dev'essere bella
Her sister must be beautiful

Dovevano essere ricchi
They must have been rich

Sua sorella doveva essere bella
Her sister must have been beautiful

Potere

The following examples will illustrate how this verb can be translated by 'to be able to', 'can', 'could', 'may' or 'might':

Posso?
May I come in?

Non possiamo leggerlo
We can't read it/We're not able to read it

Non potevano capire quel signore
They weren't able to understand that man/They couldn't understand that man

Non poteva rispondergli
She wasn't able to answer him/She couldn't answer him

Non potrai cantare quella canzone
You won't be able to sing that song

Potrei passare da te domani?
Could I (= would I be able to) pass by tomorrow?/Might I pass by tomorrow?

Potrebbe prestarmi la macchina da scrivere?
Could you (= would you be able to) lend me the typewriter?

Non potrebbe farlo
He couldn't do it/He wouldn't be able to do it

Non avrebbe potuto farlo
He couldn't have done it/He wouldn't have been able to do it

Negative & interrogative forms

Negations are made in Italian by placing *non* immediately in front of the verb. In compound tenses, the *non* is placed immediately in front of the auxiliary verb. *Do, does, did* are never translated.

> *Non capisco. Non hai finito?*
> I don't understand. Haven't you finished?

> *Non abbiamo sentito. Non avevano riposto*
> We haven't heard. They hadn't answered.

Questions

Most of the time no change in word order is made in Italian when asking a question. There is merely a change in intonation when speaking and the addition of a question mark when writing. The English *do, does, did* are never translated:

> *Parlano inglese?*
> Do they speak English?

> *Hai capito la domanda?*
> Have you understood the question?

> *Non esci stasera?*
> Aren't you going out this evening?

Sometimes questions are formed by inverting the order of the subject and predicate; it would be equally correct to keep the normal order:

> *I vostri amici arrivano alle otto?*
> or: *Arrivano alle otto i vostri amici?*
> Are your friends coming at eight?

> *I loro bambini mangiano molto?*
> or: *Mangiano molto i loro bambini?*
> Do their children eat a lot?

Irregular verbs

On pages 40–87 you will find a list of irregular verbs, those with similar irregularities being grouped together. This list does not include derivatives that are conjugated in exactly the same way as the root verb. Such derivatives will be found in the alphabetical list of all irregular Italian verbs on pages 89–95, with cross-reference numbers indicating the root verb. Thus, if you wish to know the conjugation of *soddisfare* or *rifare*, look it up under the root verb *fare* (number 4 on page 40).

INFINITIVE	GERUND & PAST PARTICIPLE	PRESENT	FUTURE -ò, -ai, -à, -emo, -ete, -anno	CONDITIONAL -ei, -esti, -ebbe, -emmo, -este, -ebbero
1. **andáre** *to go*	andando andato	vado vai va andiamo andate vanno	andr-	andr-
2. **dáre** *to give*	dando dato	do dai dà diamo date danno	dar-	dar-
3. **stáre** *to stay*	stando stato	sto stai sta stiamo state stanno	star-	star-
4. **fáre** *to make, do*	facendo fatto	faccio fai fa facciamo fate fanno	far-	far-
5. **díre** *to say, tell*	dicendo detto	dico dici dice diciamo dite dicono	dir-	dir-

IMPERFECT -o, -i, -a, -amo, -ate, -ano	PAST DEFINITE	SUBJ. PRES.	SUBJ. IMPERF. -si, -si, -se, -simo, -te, -sero
andav-	andai	vada	andas-
	andasti	vada	
	andò	vada	
	andammo	andiamo	
	andaste	andiate	
	andarono	vadano	
dav-	diedi	dia	des-
	desti	dia	
	diede	dia	
	demmo	diamo	
	deste	diate	
	diedero	diano	
stav-	stetti	stia	stes-
	stesti	stia	
	stette	stia	
	stemmo	stiamo	
	steste	stiate	
	stettero	stiano	
facev-	feci	faccia	faces-
	facesti	faccia	
	fece	faccia	
	facemmo	facciamo	
	faceste	facciate	
	fecero	facciano	
dicev-	dissi	dica	dices-
	dicesti	dica	
	disse	dica	
	dicemmo	diciamo	
	diceste	diciate	
	dissero	dicano	

INFINITIVE	GERUND & PAST PARTICIPLE	PRESENT	FUTURE -ò, -ai -à -emo, -ete, -anno	CONDITIONAL -ei, -esti, -ebbe, -emmo, -este, -ebbero
6. **piacẹre** *to like*	piacendo piaciuto	piaccio piaci piace piacciamo piacete piacciono	piacer-	piacer-
7. **tacẹre** *to keep silent*	tacendo taciuto	taccio taci tace taciamo tacete tacciono	tacer-	tacer-
8. **giacẹre** *to lie*	giacendo giaciuto	giaccio giaci giace giacciamo giacete giacciono	giacer-	giacer-
9. **trạrre** *to draw*	traendo tratto	traggo trai trae traiamo traete traggono	trarr-	trarr-
10. **cọgliere** *to gather*	cogliendo colto	colgo cogli coglie cogliamo cogliete colgono	coglier-	coglier-

IMPERFECT -o, -i, -a, -amo, -ate, -ano	PAST DEFINITE	SUBJ. PRES.	SUBJ. IMPERF. -si, -si, -se, -simo, -te, -sero
piacev-	piacqui piacesti piacque piacemmo piaceste piacquero	piaccia piaccia piaccia piacciamo piacciate piacciano	piaces-
tacev-	tacqui tacesti tacque tacemmo taceste tacquero	taccia taccia taccia tacciamo tacciate tacciano	taces-
giacev-	giacqui giacesti giacque giacemmo giaceste giacquero	giaccia giaccia giaccia giacciamo giacciate giacciano	giaces-
traev-	trassi traesti trasse traemmo traeste trassero	tragga tragga tragga traiamo traiate traggano	traes-
cogliev-	colsi cogliesti colse cogliemmo coglieste colsero	colga colga colga cogliamo cogliate colgano	coglies-

INFINITIVE	GERUND & PAST PARTICIPLE	PRESENT	FUTURE -ò, -ai, -à, -emo, -ete, -anno	CONDITIONAL -ei, -esti, -ebbe, -emmo, -este, -ebbero
11. **svęllere** *to root out*	svellendo svelto	svello svelli svelle svelliamo svellete svellono	sveller-	sveller-
12. **spęgnere** *to put out*	spegnendo spento	spengo spegni spegne spegniamo spegnete spengono	spegner-	spegner-
13. **rimanęre** *to remain*	rimanendo rimasto	rimango rimani rimane rimaniamo rimanete rimangono	rimarr-	rimarr-
14. **pǫrre** *to put*	ponendo posto	pongo poni pone poniamo ponete pongono	porr-	porr-
15. **valęre** *to be worth*	valendo valso	valgo vali vale valiamo valete valgono	varr-	varr-

IMPERFECT -o, -i, -a, -amo, -ate, -ano	PAST DEFINITE	SUBJ. PRES.	SUBJ. IMPERF. -si, -si, -se, -simo, -te, -sero
svellev-	svelsi	svella	svelles-
	svellesti	svella	
	svelse	svella	
	svellemmo	svelliamo	
	svelleste	svelliate	
	svelsero	svelliano	
spegnev-	spensi	spenga	spegnes-
	spegnesti	spenga	
	spense	spenga	
	spegnemmo	spegniamo	
	spegneste	spegniate	
	spensero	spengano	
rimanev-	rimasi	rimanga	rimanes-
	rimanesti	rimanga	
	rimase	rimanga	
	rimanemmo	rimaniamo	
	rimaneste	rimaniate	
	rimasero	rimangano	
ponev-	posi	ponga	pones-
	ponesti	ponga	
	pose	ponga	
	ponemmo	poniamo	
	poneste	poniate	
	posero	pongano	
valev-	valsi	valga	vales-
	valesti	valga	
	valse	valga	
	valemmo	valiamo	
	valeste	valiate	
	valsero	valgano	

INFINITIVE	GERUND & PAST PARTICIPLE	PRESENT	FUTURE -ò, -ai, -à, -emo, -ete, -anno	CONDITIONAL -ei, -esti, -ebbe, -emmo, -este, -ebbero
16. *salire* to ascend	salendo salito	salgo sali sale saliamo salite salgono	salir-	salir-
17. *sedere* to sit	sedendo seduto	siedo (seggo) siedi siede sediamo sedete siedono (seggono)	seder-	seder-
18. *tenere* to hold	tenendo tenuto	tengo tieni tiene teniamo tenete tengono	terr-	terr-
19. *venire* to come	venendo venuto	vengo vieni viene veniamo venite vengono	verr-	verr-
20. *dolere* to ache	dolendo dolto *or* doluto	dolgo duoli duole dogliamo dolete dolgono	dorr-	dorr-

46

IMPERFECT -o, -i, -a, -amo, -ate, -ano	PAST DEFINITE	SUBJ. PRES.	SUBJ. IMPERF. -si, -si, -se, -simo, -te, -sero
saliv-	salii	salga	salis-
	salisti	salga	
	salì	salga	
	salimmo	saliamo	
	saliste	saliate	
	salirono	salgano	
sedev-	sedei	sieda	sedes-
	sedesti	sieda	
	sedé (sedette)	sieda	
	sedemmo	sediamo	
	sedeste	sediate	
	sederono	siedano	
	(sedettero)	(seggano)	
tenev-	tenni	tenga	tenes-
	tenesti	tenga	
	tenne	tenga	
	tenemmo	teniamo	
	teneste	teniate	
	tennero	tengano	
veniv-	venni	venga	venis-
	venisti	venga	
	venne	venga	
	venimmo	veniamo	
	veniste	veniate	
	vennero	vengano	
dolev-	dolsi	dolga	doles-
	dolesti	dolga	
	dolse	dolga	
	dolemmo	dogliamo	
	doleste	dogliate	
	dolsero	dolgano	

INFINITIVE	GERUND & PAST PARTICIPLE	PRESENT	FUTURE -ò, -ai, -à, -emo, -ete, -anno	CONDITIONAL -ei, -esti, -ebbe, -emmo, -este, -ebbero
21. **solęre** *to be used*	solendo solito	soglio suoli suole sogliamo solete sogliono	—	—
22. **volęre** *to want*	volendo voluto	voglio vuoi vuole vogliamo volete vogliono	vorr-	vorr-
23. **potęre** *to be able, may, can*	potendo potuto	posso puoi può possiamo potete possono	potr-	potr-
24. **nuǫcere** *to hurt, harm*	nuocendo nociuto	nuoccio (noccio) nuoci nuoce nociamo nocete nuocciono (nocciono)	nuocer-	nuocer-
25. **cuǫcere** *to cook*	cuocendo cotto	cuocio cuoci cuoce cociamo cocete cuociono	cuocer-	cuocer-

IMPERFECT -o, -i, -a, -amo, -ate, -ano	PAST DEFINITE	SUBJ. PRES.	SUBJ. IMPERF. -si, -si, -se, -simo, -te, -sero
solev-	solei	soglia	soles-
	solesti	soglia	
	solé	soglia	
	solemmo	sogliamo	
	soleste	sogliate	
	solerono	sogliano	
volev-	volli	voglia	voles-
	volesti	voglia	
	volle	voglia	
	volemmo	vogliamo	
	voleste	vogliate	
	vollero	vogliano	
potev-	potei	possa	potes-
	potesti	possa	
	poté	possa	
	potemmo	possiamo	
	poteste	possiate	
	poterono	possano	
nuocev-	nocqui	noccia	nuoces-
	nocesti	noccia	
	nocque	noccia	
	nocemmo	nocciamo	
	noceste	nocciate	
	noquero	nocciano	
cuocev-	cossi	cuocia	cuoces-
	cocesti	cuocia	
	cosse	cuocia	
	cocemmo	cociamo	
	coceste	cociate	
	cossero	cuociano	

49

INFINITIVE	GERUND & PAST PARTICIPLE	PRESENT	FUTURE -ò, -ai, -à, -emo, -ete, -anno	CONDITIONAL -ei, -esti, -ebbe, -emmo, -este, -ebbero
26. **muovere** *to move*	muovendo mosso	muovo muovi muove moviamo movete muovono	muover-	muover-
27. **scuotere** *to shake*	scuotendo scosso	scuoto scuoti scuote scotiamo scotete scuotono	scuoter-	scuoter-
28. **morire** *to die*	morendo morto	muoio muori muore moriamo morite muoiono	morir- *or* morr-	morir- *or* morr-
29. **udire** *to hear*	udendo udito	odo odi ode udiamo udite odono	udir-	udir-
30. **uscire** *to go out*	uscendo uscito	esco esci esce usciamo uscite escono	uscir-	uscir-

IMPERFECT -o, -i, -a, -amo, -ate, -ano	PAST DEFINITE	SUBJ. PRES.	SUBJ. IMPERF. -si, -si, -se, -simo, -te, -sero
muovev-	mossi	muova	muoves-
	movesti	muova	
	mosse	muova	
	movemmo	muoviamo	
	moveste	muoviate	
	mossero	muovano	
scuotev-	scossi	scuota	scuotes-
	scotesti	scuota	
	scosse	scuota	
	scotemmo	scuotiamo	
	scoteste	scuotiate	
	scossero	scuotano	
moriv-	morii	muoia	moris-
	moristi	muoia	
	morì	muoia	
	morimmo	muoiamo	
	moriste	muoiate	
	morirono	muoiano	
udiv-	udii	oda	udis-
	udisti	oda	
	udì	oda	
	udimmo	udiamo	
	udiste	udiate	
	udirono	odano	
usciv-	uscii	esca	uscis-
	uscisti	esca	
	uscì	esca	
	uscimmo	usciamo	
	usciste	usciate	
	uscirono	escano	

INFINITIVE	GERUND & PAST PARTICIPLE	PRESENT	FUTURE -ò, -ai, -à, -emo, -ete, -anno	CONDITIONAL -ei, -esti, -ebbe, -emmo, -este, -ebbero
31. **dovére** *to have to, must*	dovendo dovuto	devo (debbo) devi deve dobbiamo dovete devono (debbono)	dovr-	dovr-
32. **parére** *to seem*	parendo parso	paio pari pare paiamo parete paiono	parr-	parr-
33. **apparire** *to appear*	apparendo apparso	appaio (apparisco) appari (apparisci) appare (apparisce) appariamo apparite appaiono (appariscono)	apparir-	apparir-

IMPERFECT -o, -i, -a, -amo, -ate, -ano	PAST DEFINITE	SUBJ. PRES.	SUBJ. IMPERF. -si, -si, -se, -simo, -te, -sero
dovev-	dovei (dovetti) dovesti dové (dovette) dovemmo doveste doverono (dovettero)	debba (deva) debba (deva) debba (deva) dobbiamo dobbiate debbano (devano)	doves-
parev-	parvi paresti parve paremmo pareste parvero	paia paia paia paiamo paiate paiano	pares-
appariv-	apparvi apparisti apparve apparimmo appariste apparvero	apparisca apparisca apparisca appariamo appariate appariscano	apparis-

INFINITIVE	GERUND & PAST PARTICIPLE	PRESENT -o, -i, -e, -iamo, -ete, -ono	FUTURE -ò, -ai, -à, -emo, -ete, -anno	CONDITIONAL -ei, -esti, -ebbe, -emmo, -este, -ebbero
34. **persuadere** *to persuade*	persuadendo persuaso	persuad-	persuader-	persuader-
35. **evadere** *to evade*	evadendo evaso	evad-	evader-	evader-
36. **radere** *to shave*	radendo raso	rad-	rader-	rader-
37. **ledere** *to hurt, offend*	ledendo leso	led-	leder-	leder-
38. **elidere** *to elide*	elidendo eliso	elid-	elider-	elider-
39. **chiedere** *to ask*	chiedendo chiesto	chied-	chieder-	chieder-
40. **conquidere** *to win*	conquidendo conquiso	conquid-	conquider-	conquider-
41. **decidere** *to decide*	decidendo deciso	decid-	decider-	decider-
42. **uccidere** *to kill*	uccidendo ucciso	uccid-	uccider-	uccider-
43. **ridere** *to laugh*	ridendo riso	rid-	rider-	rider-
44. **assidersi** *to sit*	assidendosi assiso	mi assid-	mi assider-	mi assider-

IMPERFECT -o, -i, -a, -amo, -ate, -ano	PAST DEFINITE -si, -desti, -se, -demmo, -deste, -sero	SUBJ. PRES. -a, -a, -a, -iamo, -iate, -ano	SUBJ. IMPERF. -essi, -essi, -esse, -essimo, -este, -essero
persuadev-	persua-	persuad-	persuad-
evadev-	eva-	evad-	evad-
radev-	ra-	rad-	rad-
ledev-	le-	led-	led-
elidev-	eli-	elid-	elid-
chiedev-	chie-	chied-	chied-
conquidev-	conqui-	conquid-	conquid-
decidev-	deci-	decid-	decid-
uccidev-	ucci-	uccid-	uccid-
ridev-	ri-	rid-	rid-
mi assidev-	mi assi-	mi assid-	mi assid-

55

INFINITIVE	GERUND & PAST PARTICIPLE	PRESENT -o, -i, -e, -iamo, -ete, -ono	FUTURE -ò, -ai, -à, -emo, -ete, -anno	CONDITIONAL -ei, -esti, -ebbe, -emmo, -este, -ebbero
45. **divịdere** *to divide*	dividendo diviso	divid-	divider-	divider-
46. **intrịdere** *to temper*	intridendo intriso	intrid-	intrider-	intrider-
47. **rọdere** *to gnaw*	rodendo roso	rod-	roder-	roder-
48. **esplọdere** *to explode*	esplodendo esploso	esplod-	esploder-	esploder-
49. **chiụdere** *to close*	chiudendo chiuso	chiud-	chiuder-	chiuder-
50. **acclụdere** *to enclose*	accludendo accluso	acclud-	accluder-	accluder-
51. **allụdere** *to allude*	alludendo alluso	allud-	alluder-	alluder-
52. intrụdere *to intrude*	intrudendo intruso	intrud-	intruder-	intruder-
53. **spạndere** *to spill*	spandendo spanto	spand-	spander-	spander-

IMPERFECT -o, -i, -a, -amo, -ate, -ano	PAST DEFINITE -si, -desti, -se, -demmo, -desto, -sero	SUBJ. PRES. -a, -a, -a, -iamo, -iate, -ano	SUBJ. IMPERF. -essi, -essi, -esse, -essimo, -este, -essero
dividev-	divi-	divid-	divid-
intridev-	intri-	intrid-	intrid-
rodev-	ro-	rod-	rod-
esplodev-	esplo-	esplod-	esplod-
chiudev-	chiu-	chiud-	chiud-
accludev-	acclu-	acclud-	acclud-
alludev-	allu-	allud-	allud-
intrudev-	intru-	intrud-	intrud-
spandev-	span-	spand-	spand-

INFINITIVE	GERUND & PAST PARTICIPLE	PRESENT -o, -i, -e, -iamo, -ete, -ono	FUTURE -ò, -ai, -à, -emo, -ete, -anno	CONDITIONAL -ei, -esti, -ebbe, -emmo, -este, -ebbero
54. **accęndere** to light	accendendo acceso	accend-	accender-	accender-
55. **difęndere** to defend	difendendo difeso	difend-	difender-	difender-
56. **appęndere** to hang	appendendo appeso	append-	appender-	appender-
57. **pręndere** to take	prendendo preso	prend-	prender-	prender-
58. **ręndere** to render	rendendo reso	rend-	render-	render-
59. **scęndere** to descend	scendendo sceso	scend-	scender-	scender-
60. **tęndere** to tend	tendendo teso	tend-	tender-	tender-
61. **rispọndere** to answer, reply	rispondendo risposto	rispond-	risponder-	risponder-
62. **nascọndere** to hide	nascondendo nascosto	nascond-	nasconder-	nasconder-
63. **fọndere** to melt	fondendo fuso	fond-	fonder-	fonder-

IMPERFECT	PAST DEFINITE	SUBJ. PRES.	SUBJ. IMPERF.
-o, -i,	-si, -ndesti,	-a, -a, -a,	-essi, -essi,
-a,	-se, -ndemmo,	-iamo,	-esse,
-amo, -ate,	-ndeste,	-iate,	-essimo,
-ano	-sero	-ano	-este, -essero
accendev-	acce-	accend-	accend-
difendev-	dife-	difend-	difend-
appendev-	appe-	append-	append-
prendev-	pre-	prend-	prend-
rendev-	re-	rend-	rend-
scendev-	sce-	scend-	scend-
tendev-	te-	tend-	tend-
rispondev-	rispo-	rispond-	rispond-
nascondev-	nasco-	nascond-	nascond-
fondev-	fusi fondesti fuse fondemmo fondeste fusero	fond-	fond-

INFINITIVE	GERUND & PAST PARTICIPLE	PRESENT -o, -i, -e, -iamo, -ete, -ono	FUTURE -ò, -ai, -à, -emo, -ete, -anno	CONDITIONAL -ei, -esti, -ebbe, -emmo, -este, -ebbero
64. **contundere** *to bruise*	contundendo contuso	contund-	contunder-	contunder-
65. **ardere** *to burn*	ardendo arso	ard-	arder-	arder-
66. **perdere** *to lose*	perdendo perso	perd-	perder-	perder-
67. **mordere** *to bite*	mordendo morso	mord-	morder-	morder-
68. **piangere** *to cry*	piangendo pianto	piang-	pianger-	pianger-
69. **frangere** *to break*	frangendo franto	frang-	franger-	franger-
70. **attingere** *to draw*	attingendo attinto	atting-	attinger-	attinger-
71. **cingere** *to gird*	cingendo cinto	cing-	cinger-	cinger-
72. **fingere** *to feign, pretend*	fingendo finto	fing-	finger-	finger-

IMPERFECT -o, -i, -a, -amo, -ate, -ano	PAST DEFINITE -si, -ndesti, -se, -ndemmo, -ndeste, -sero	SUBJ. PRES. -a, -a, -a, -iamo, -iate, -ano	SUBJ. IMPERF. -essi, -essi, -esse, -essimo, -este, -essero
contundev-	contu- ———————— -si, -desti, -se, -demmo, -deste, -sero:	contund-	contund-
ardev-	ar-	ard-	ard-
perdev-	per-	perd-	perd-
mordev-	mor- ———————— -si, -gesti, -se, -gemmo, -geste, -sero:	mord-	mord-
piangev-	pian-	piang-	piang-
frangev-	fran-	frang-	frang-
attingev-	attin-	atting-	atting-
cingev-	cing-	cing-	cing-
fingev-	fin-	fing-	fing-

INFINITIVE	GERUND & PAST PARTICIPLE	PRESENT -o, -i, -e, -iamo, -ete, -ono	FUTURE -ò, -ai, -à, -emo, -ete, -anno	CONDITIONAL -ei, -esti, -ebbe, -emmo, -este, -ebbero
73. **dipingere** *to paint*	dipingendo dipinto	diping-	**dipinger-**	dipinger-
74. **spingere** *to push*	spingendo spinto	sping-	**spinger-**	spinger-
75. **tingere** *to dye*	tingendo tinto	ting-	**tinger-**	tinger-
76. **distinguere** *to distinguish*	distinguendo distinto	distingu-	**distinguer-**	distinguer-
77. **fungere** *to act as*	fundendo	fung-	**funger-**	funger-
78. **giungere** *to arrive*	giungendo giunto	giung-	**giunger-**	giunger-
79. **mungere** *to milk*	mungendo munto	mung-	**munger-**	munger-
80. **pungere** *to sting*	pungendo punto	pung-	**punger-**	punger-
81. **ungere** *to grease*	ungendo unto	ung-	**unger-**	unger-
82. **spargere** *to spread, scatter*	spargendo sparso	sparg-	**sparger-**	sparger-

IMPERFECT -o, -i, -a, -amo, -ate, -ano	PAST DEFINITE -si, -gesti, -se, -gemmo, -geste, -sero	SUBJ. PRES. -a, -a, -a -iamo, -iate, -ano	SUBJ. IMPERF. -essi, -essi, -esse, -essimo, -este, -essero
dipingev-	dipin-	diping-	diping-
spingev-	spin-	sping-	sping-
tingev-	tin-	ting-	ting-
distinguev-	distinsti distinguesti distinse distinguemmo distingueste distinsero	distingu-	distingu-
fungev-	fun-	fung-	fung-
giungev-	giun-	giung-	giung-
mungev-	mun-	mung-	mung-
pungev-	pun-	pung-	pung-
ungev-	un-	ung-	ung-
spargev-	spar-	sparg-	sparg-

INFINITIVE	GERUND & PAST PARTICIPLE	PRESENT -o, -i, -e, -iamo, -ete, -ono	FUTURE -ò, -ai, -à, -emo, -ete, -anno	CONDITIONAL -ei, -esti, -ebbe, -emmo, -este, -ebbero
83. **aspergere** *to sprinkle*	aspergendo asperso	asperg-	asperger-	asperger-
84. **emergere** *to emerge*	emergendo emerso	emerg-	emerger-	emerger-
85. **ergere** *to erect*	ergendo erto	erg-	erger-	erger-
86. **accorgersi** *to realize, notice*	accorgendosi accorto	mi accorg-	mi accorger-	mi accorger-
87. **porgere** *to offer, give*	porgendo porto	porg-	porger-	porger-
88. **sorgere** *to arise*	sorgendo sorto	sorg-	sorger-	sorger-
89. **tergere** *to clean, wipe*	tergendo terso	**terg-**	**terger-**	terger-
90. **convergere** *to converge*	convergendo converso	**converg-**	**converger-**	converger-
91. **indulgere** *to indulge*	indulgendo indulto	**indulg-**	indulger-	indulger-
92. **volgere** *to turn*	volgendo volto	volg-	volger-	volger-

IMPERFECT -o, -i, -a, -amo, -ate, -ano	PAST DEFINITE -si, -gesti, -se, -gemmo, -geste, -sero	SUBJ. PRES. -a, -a, -a, -iamo, -iate, -ano	SUBJ. IMPERF. -essi, -essi, -esse, -essimo, -este, -essero
aspergev-	asper-	asperg-	asperg-
emergev-	emer-	emerg-	emerg-
ergev-	er-	**erg-**	**erg-**
mi accorgev-	mi accor-	mi accor-	mi accor-
porgev-	por-	porg-	porg-
sorgev-	sor-	sorg-	sorg-
tergev-	ter-	terg-	terg-
convergev-	conver-	converg-	converg-
indulgev-	indul-	**indulg-**	**indulg-**
volgev-	vol-	**volg-**	volg-

INFINITIVE	GERUND & PAST PARTICIPLE	PRESENT -o, -i, -e, -iamo, -ete, -ono	FUTURE -ò, -ai, -à, -emo, -ete, -anno	CONDITIONAL -ei, -esti, -ebbe, -emmo, -este, -ebbero
93. *vincere* to win	vincendo vinto	vinc-	vincer-	vincer-
94. *torcere* to twist	torcendo torto	torc-	torcer-	torcer-
95. *espellere* to expel	espellendo espulso	espell-	espeller-	espeller-
96. *eccellere* to excel	eccellendo eccelso	eccell-	ecceller-	ecceller-

		-o, -i, -e, -iamo, -ite, -ono		
97. *aprire* to open	aprendo aperto	apr-	aprir-	aprir-
98. *coprire* to cover	coprendo coperto	copr-	coprir-	coprir-
99. *offrire* to offer	offrendo offerto	offr-	offrir-	offrir-
100. *soffrire* to suffer	soffrendo sofferto	soffr-	soffrir-	soffrir-

IMPERFECT -o, -i, -a, -amo, -ate, -ano	PAST DEFINITE -si, -cesti, -se, -cemmo, -ceste, -sero	SUBJ. PRES. -a, -a, -a, -iamo, -iate, -ano	SUBJ. IMPERF. -essi, -essi, -esse, -essimo, -este, -essero
vincev-	vin-	vinc-	vinc-
torcev-	tor-	**torc-**	**torc-**
espellev-	espulsi espellesti espulse espellemmo espelleste espulsero	**espell-**	espell-
eccellev-	eccelsi eccellesti eccelse eccellemmo eccelleste eccelsero	eccell-	eccell-
	-ii, -isti, -ì, -immo, -iste, -irono		-issi, -issi, -isse, -issimo, -iste, -issero
apriv-	apersi *or* apr-	apr-	apr-
copriv-	copersi *or* copr-	copr-	copr-
offriv-	offersi *or* offr-	offr-	offr-
soffriv-	soffersi *or* soffr-	**soffr-**	soffr-

INFINITIVE	GERUND & PAST PARTICIPLE	PRESENT -isco, -isci, -isce, -iamo, -ite, -iscono	FUTURE -ò, -ai, -à, -emo, -ete, -anno	CONDITIONAL -ei, -esti, -ebbe, -emmo, -este, -ebbero
101. **proferire** *to utter*	proferendo proferito	profer-	proferir-	proferir-
102. **inferire** *to infer*	inferendo inferto *or* inferito	infer-	inferir-	inferir-

		PRESENT -o, -i, -e, -iamo, -ete, -ono		
103. **correre** *to run*	correndo corso	corr-	correr-	correr-
104. **redimere** *to redeem*	redimendo redento	redim-	**redimer-**	**redimer-**
105. **assumere** *to assume*	assumendo assunto	**assum-**	assumer-	assumer-

IMPERFECT	PAST DEFINITE	SUBJ. PRES.	SUBJ. IMPERF.
-o, -i,	-ii, -isti,	-sca, -sca,	-issi, -issi,
-a,	-ì, -immo,	-sca,	-isse,
-amo, -ate,	-iste,	-amo, -ate,	-issimo,
-ano	-irono	-scano	-iste, -issero

proferiv-	profersi *or* profer-	proferi-	profer-
inferiv-	infer-	inferi-	infer-

		-a, -a, -a,	-essi, -essi,
		-iamo,	-esse,
		-iate,	-essimo,
		-ano	-este, -essero
correv-	corsi corrresti corse corremmo correste corsero	corr-	corr-
redimev-	redensi redimesti redense redimemmo redimeste redensero	redim-	redim-
assumev-	assunsi assumesti assunse assumemmo assumeste assunsero	assum-	assum-

INFINITIVE	GERUND & PAST PARTICIPLE	PRESENT -o, -i, -e, -iamo, -ete, -ono	FUTURE -ò, -ai, -à, -emo, -ete, -anno	CONDITIONAL -ei, -esti, -ebbe, -emmo, -este, -ebbero
106. **mettere** *to put*	mettendo messo	mett-	metter-	metter-
107. **dirigere** *to direct*	dirigendo diretto	dirig-	diriger-	diriger-
108. **redigere** *to write*	redigendo redatto	redig-	rediger-	rediger-
109. **esigere** *to exact, require*	esigendo esatto	esig-	esiger-	esiger-
110. **affliggere** *to afflict*	affliggendo afflitto	affligg-	affligger-	affligger-

IMPERFECT -o, -i, -a, -amo, -ate, -ano	PAST DEFINITE	SUBJ. PRES. -a, -a, -a, -iamo, -iate, -ano	SUBJ. IMPERF. -essi, -essi, -esse, -essimo, -este, -essero
mettev-	misi mettesti mise mettemmo metteste misero	mett-	mett-
dirigev-	diressi dirigesti diresse dirigemmo dirigeste diressero	dirig-	dirig-
redigev-	redassi redigesti redasse redigemmo redigeste redassero	**redig-**	redig-
esigev-	esigei (esigetti) esigesti esigé (-ette) esigemmo esigeste esigerono (esigettero)	esig-	esig-
affliggev-	afflissi affliggesti afflisse affliggemmo affliggeste afflissero	affligg-	affligg-

INFINITIVE	GERUND & PAST PARTICIPLE	PRESENT -o, -i, -e, -iamo, -ete, -ono	FUTURE -ò, -ai, -à, -emo, -ete, -anno	CONDITIONAL -ei, -esti, -ebbe, -emmo, -este, -ebbero
111. **figgere** *to fix*	figgendo fitto	figg-	figger-	figger-
112. **affiggere** *to stick*	affiggendo affisso	affigg-	affigger-	affigger-
113. **friggere** *to fry*	friggendo fritto	frigg-	frigger-	frigger-
114. **leggere** *to read*	leggendo letto	legg-	legger-	legger-
115. **negligere** *to neglect*	negligendo negletto	neglig-	negliger-	negliger-

IMPERFECT -o, -i, -a, -amo, -ate, -ano	PAST DEFINITE	SUBJ. PRES. -a, -a, -a, -iamo, -iate, -ano	SUBJ. IMPERF. -essi, -essi, -esse, -essimo, -este, -essero
figgev-	fissi figgesti fisse figgemmo figgeste fissero	figg-	figg-
affiggev-	affissi affiggesti affisse affiggemmo affiggeste affissero	affigg-	affig-
friggev-	frissi friggesti frisse friggemmo friggeste frissero	frigg-	frigg-
leggev-	lessi leggesti lesse leggemmo leggeste lessero	legg-	legg-
negligev-	neglessi negligesti neglesse negligemmo negligeste neglessero	neglig-	neglig-

INFINITIVE	GERUND & PAST PARTICIPLE	PRESENT -o, -i, -e, -iamo, -ete, -ono	FUTURE -ò, -ai, -à, -emo, -ete, -anno	CONDITIONAL -ei, -esti, -ebbe, -emmo, -este, -ebbero
116. **prediligere** *to prefer*	prediligendo prediletto	predilig-	prediliger-	prediliger-
117. **proteggere** *to protect*	proteggendo protetto	protegg-	protegger-	protegger-
118. **reggere** *to support*	reggendo retto	regg-	regger-	regger-
119. **struggere** *to consume*	struggendo strutto	strugg-	strugger-	strugger-
120. **riflettere** *to reflect*	riflettendo riflesso	riflett-	rifletter-	rifletter-

IMPERFECT -o, -i, -a, -amo, -ate, -ano	PAST DEFINITE	SUBJ. PRES. -a, -a, -a, -iamo, -iate, -ano	SUBJ. IMPERF. -essi, -essi, -esse, -essimo, -este, -essero
prediligev-	predilessi prediligesti predilesse prediligemmo prediligeste predilessero	predilig-	predilig-
proteggev-	protessi proteggesti protesse proteggemmo proteggeste protessero	protegg-	protegg-
reggev-	ressi reggesti resse reggemmo reggeste ressero	regg-	regg-
struggev-	strussi struggesti strusse struggemmo struggeste strussero	strugg-	strugg-
riflettev-	riflessi riflettesti riflesse riflettemmo rifletteste riflessero	riflett-	riflett-

INFINITIVE	GERUND & PAST PARTICIPLE	PRESENT -o, -i, -e, -iamo, -ete, -ono	FUTURE -ò, -ai, -à, -emo, -ete, -anno	CONDITIONAL -ei, -esti, -ebbe, -emmo, -este, -ebbero
121. **genuflĕttersi** *to genuflect*	genuflettendosi genuflesso	mi etc. genuflett-	mi etc. genufletter-	mi etc. genufletter-
122. **annĕttere** *to annex*	annettendo annesso	annett-	annetter-	annetter-
123. **discŭtere** *to discuss*	discutendo discusso	discut-	discuter-	discuter-
124. **condŭrre** *to lead, drive*	conducendo condotto	conduc-	condurr-	condurr-
125. **scrĭvere** *to write*	scrivendo scritto	scriv-	scriver-	scriver-

IMPERFECT -o, -i, -a, -amo, -ate, -ano	PAST DEFINITE	SUBJ. PRES. -a, -a, -a, -iamo, -iate, -ano	SUBJ. IMPERF. -essi, -essi, -esse, -essimo, -este, -essero
mi etc. genuflettev-	mi etc. genuflessi genuflettesti genuflesse genuflettemmo genufletteste genuflessero	mi etc. genuflett-	mi etc. genuflett-
annettev-	annessi annettesti annesse annettemmo annetteste annessero	annett-	annett-
discutev-	discussi discutesti discusse discutemmo discuteste discussero	discut-	discut-
conducev-	condussi conducesti condusse conducemmo conduceste condussero	conduc-	conduc-
scrivev-	scrissi scrivesti scrisse scrivemmo scriveste scrissero	scriv-	scriv-

INFINITIVE	GERUND & PAST PARTICIPLE	PRESENT -o, -i, -e, -iamo, -ete, -ono	FUTURE -ò, -ai, -à, -emo, -ete, -anno	CONDITIONAL -ei, -esti, -ebbe, -emmo, -este, -ebbero
126. **vívere** *to live*	vivendo vissuto	viv-	vivr-	vivr-
127. **costruíre** *to build, construct*	costruendo costruito	costruisco costruisci costruisce costruiamo costruite costruiscono	costruir-	costruir-
128. **esprímere** *to express*	esprimendo espresso	esprim-	esprimer-	esprimer-
129. **scíndere** *to separate*	scindendo scisso	scind-	scinder-	scinder-
130. **concédere** *to concede*	concedendo concesso *or* conceduto	conced-	conceder-	conceder-

IMPERFECT -o, -i, -a, -amo, -ate, -ano	PAST DEFINITE	SUBJ. PRES. -a, -a, -a, -iamo, -iate, -ano	SUBJ. IMPERF. -essi, -essi -esse, -essimo, -este, -essero
vivev-	vissi vivesti visse vivemmo viveste vissero	viv-	viv-
costruiv-	costruii (costrussi) costruisti costruì costruimmo costruiste costruirono	costruisc-	costruissi costruissi costruisse costruissimo costruiste costruissero
esprimev-	espressi esprimesti espresse esprimemmo esprimeste espressero	esprim-	esprim-
scindev-	scissi scindesti scisse scindemmo scindeste scissero	scind-	scind-
concedev-	concessi concedesti concesse concedemmo concedeste concessero	conced-	conced-

INFINITIVE	GERUND & PAST PARTICIPLE	PRESENT -o, -i, -e, -iamo, -ete, -ono	FUTURE -ò, -ai, -à, -emo, -ete, -anno	CONDITIONAL -ei, -esti, -ebbe, -emmo, -este, -ebbero
131. **nascere** *to be born*	nascendo nato	nasc-	nascer-	nascer-
132. **bere** *to drink*	bevendo bevuto	bev-	berr-	berr-
133. **piovere** *to rain*	piovendo piovuto	piov-	piover-	piover-
134. **crescere** *to grow*	crescendo cresciuto	cresc-	crescer-	crescer-
135. **conoscere** *to know*	conoscendo conosciuto	conosc-	conoscer-	conoscer-

IMPERFECT -o, -i, -a, -amo, -ate, -ano	PAST DEFINITE	SUBJ. PRES. -a, -a, -a, -iamo, -iate, -ano	SUBJ. IMPERF. -essi, -essi, -esse, -essimo, -este, -essero
nascev-	nacqui nascesti nacque nascemmo nasceste nacquero	nasc-	nasc-
bevev-	bevvi bevesti bevve bevemmo beveste bevvero	bev-	bev-
piovev-	piovvi piovesti piovve piovemmo pioveste piovvero	piov-	piov-
crescev-	crebbi crescesti crebbe crescemmo cresceste crebbero	cresc-	cresc-
conoscev-	conobbi conoscesti conobbe conoscemmo conocsceste conobbero	conosc-	conosc-

INFINITIVE	GERUND & PAST PARTICIPLE	PRESENT -o, -i, -e, -iamo, -ete, -ono	FUTURE -ò, -ai, -à, -emo, -ete, -anno	CONDITIONAL -ei, -esti, -ebbe, -emmo, -este, -ebbero
136. *cadęre* *to fall*	cadendo caduto	cad-	cadr-	cadr-
137. *rǫmpere* *to break*	rompendo rotto	romp-	romper-	romper-
138. *vedęre* *to see*	vedendo veduto	ved-	vedr-	vedr-
138b. *assįstere* *to be present at*	assistendo assistito	assist-	assister-	assister-
139. *devǫlvere* *to devolve*	devolvendo devoluto	devolv-	devolver-	devolver-

IMPERFECT -o, -i, -a, -amo, -ate, -ano	PAST DEFINITE	SUBJ. PRES. -a, -a, -a, -iamo, -iate, -ano	SUBJ. IMPERF. -essi, -essi, -esse, -essimo, -este, -essero
cadev-	caddi cadesti cadde cademmo cadeste caddero	cad-	cad-
rompev-	ruppi rompesti ruppe rompemmo rompeste ruppero	romp-	romp-
vedev-	vidi vedesti vide vedemmo vedeste videro	ved-	ved-
assistev-	assistei assistesti assisté assistemmo assisteste assisterono		
devolvev-	devolvei (devolvetti) devolvesti devolvé dovolvemmo devolveste devolverono (devolvettero)	devolv-	devolv-

INFINITIVE	GERUND & PAST PARTICIPLE	PRESENT -o, -i, -e, -iamo, -ete, -ono	FUTURE -ò, -ai, -à, -emo, -ete, -anno	CONDITIONAL -ei, -esti -ebbe, -emmo, -este, -ebbero
140. **seppelire** *to bury*	seppellendo sepolto *or* seppellito	seppellisco seppellisci seppellisce seppelliamo sepellite seppelliscono	seppellir-	seppellir-
141. **assolvere** *to absolve*	assolvendo assolto	assolv-	assolver-	assolver-
142. **sapere** *to know*	sapendo saputo	so sai sa sappiamo sapete sanno	sapr-	sapr-
143. **godere** *to enjoy*	godendo goduto	god-	godr-	godr-
144. **stringere** *to draw close*	stringendo stretto	string-	stringer-	stringer-

IMPERFECT -o, -i, -a, -amo, -ate, -ano	PAST DEFINITE	SUBJ. PRES. -a, -a, -a -iamo, -iate, -ano	SUBJ. IMPERF. -essi, -essi, -esse, -essimo, -este, -essero
seppelliv-	seppellii seppellisti seppellì seppellimmo seppelliste seppellirono	seppellisc-	seppellissi seppellissi seppellisse seppellissimo seppelliste seppellissero
assolvev-	assolsi assolvesti assolvé assolvemmo assolveste assolsero	assolv-	assolv-
sapev-	seppi sapesti seppe sappemmo sapeste seppero	sappia sappia sappia sappiamo sappiate sappiano	sap-
godev-	godei (godetti) godesti godé (godette) godemmo godeste goderono (godettero)	god-	god-
stringev-	strinsi stringesti strinse stringemmo stringeste strinsero	string-	string-

INFINITIVE	GERUND & PAST PARTICIPLE	PRESENT -o, -i, -e, -iamo, -ete, -ono	FUTURE -ò, -ai, -à, -emo, -ete, -anno	CONDITIONAL -ei, -esti, -ebbe, -emmo, -este, -ebbero
145. **rifulgere** *to shine*	rifulgendo rifulso	rifulg-	rifulger-	rifulger-
146. **scegliere** *to choose*	scegliendo scelto	scelgo scegli sceglie scegliamo scegliete scelgono	sceglier-	scelgier-
147. **sciogliere** *to melt, dissolve*	sciogliendo sciolto	sciolgo sciogli scioglie sciogliamo sciogliete sciolgono	scioglier-	scioglier-
148. **togliere** *to take from*	togliendo tolto	tolgo togli toglie togliamo togliete tolgono	toglier-	toglier-

149. **propendere** (*to incline*) is conjugated like a regular *-ere* verb, except in the past participle, which is propenso.

150. **assorbire** (*to absorb*) is conjugated like a regular *-ire* verb (present indicative: assorbo or assorbisco), but it has two past participles, assorbito and assorto.

151. **inserire** (*to insert*) is conjugated like a regular *-ire* verb, but it has two past participles, inserito and inserto.

IMPERFECT -o, -i, -a, -amo, -ate, -amo	PAST DEFINITE	SUBJ. PRES. -a, -a, -a, -iamo, -iate, -ano	SUBJ. IMPERF. -essi, -essi, -esse, -essimo, -este, -essero
rifulgev-	rifulsi rifulgesti rifulse rifulgemmo rifulgeste rifulsero	rifulg-	rifulg-
scegliev-	scelsi scegliesti scelse scegliemmo sceglieste scelsero	scelga scelga scelga scegliamo scegliate scelgano	scegli-
sciogliev-	sciolsi sciogliesti sciolse sciogliemmo scioglieste sciolsero	sciolga sciolga sciolga sciogliamo sciogliate sciolgano	sciogli-
togliev-	tolsi toglieste tolse togliemmo toglieste tolsero	tolga tolga tolga togliamo togliate tolgano	togli-

Defective verbs

The following verbs have only the persons and tenses given:

152. **aggradąre** *to like*

Impersonal; used only in the present indicative: *mi aggrada, ti aggrada,* etc.

153. **calęre** *to matter*

Obsolete, except in the present indicative: *mi cale* (it matters to me), *ti cale* (it matters to you), etc.

154. **lįcere** *to be permitted*

Past participle: *lecito* (permitted); present indicative: *lice* (it is permitted).

155. **molcęre** *to soothe, mitigate*

Used only in poetry. Gerund: *molcendo,* present indic.: *molce* (it soothes); imperfect: *molceva.*

156. **rilųcere** *to shine*

Present ind.: *riluce, rilucono;* imperfect ind.: *riluceva, rilucevano.*

157. **ųrgere** *to be urgent*

Impersonal. Gerund: *urgendo;* pres. ind.: *urge;* imperfect: *urgeva;* present subjunctive: *urga;* imp. subjunct.: *urgesse.*

158. **vįgere** *to be in force*

Gerund: *vigendo;* pres. ind.: *vige, vigono;* imperf. ind.: *vigeva, vigevano;* imp. subjunct.: *vigesse, vigessero.*

159. **concęrnere** *to concern*

Impersonal. Pres. ind.: *concerne;* imperf. ind.: *concerneva;* imperf. subjunct.: *concernesse.*

160. **esįmersi** *to withdraw from*

Conjugated like a regular -ere verb, but it has neither a past definite nor a past participle.

161. **fęrvere** *to be hot*

Gerund: *fervendo;* pres. ind.: *ferve;* imperf. ind.: *ferveva;* imperf. subjunct.: *fervesse.*

162. **splęndere** *to shine*

A regular -ere verb, but it has no past participle.

Alphabetical list of irregular verbs

The number after the verb refers you to the appropriate model or root verb in the previous section.

accadére *to happen*	136	assorbíre *to absorb*	150
accédere *to accede*	130	assúmere *to assume*	105
accéndere *to light, switch on*	54	astenérsi *to abstain*	18
acclúdere *to enclose*	50	astrárre *to abstract*	9
accógliere *to receive, welcome*	10	atténdere *to wait for*	60
accórgersi *to realize, notice*	86	attíngere *to draw up*	70
accórrere *to run up to*	103	avvedérsi *to notice*	138
accréscere *to increase*	134	avveníre *to happen*	19
addírsi *to suit*	5	avvíncere *to tie up, unite*	93
addúrre *to convey*	124	avvólgere *to fold*	92
affíggere *to stick*	112	benedíre *to bless*	5
afflíggere *to afflict*	110	bére *to drink*	132
aggiúngere *to add*	78	cadére *to fall*	136
aggradáre *to like*	152	calére *to matter*	153
allúdere *to allude*	51	chiédere *to ask*	39
amméttere *to admit*	106	chiúdere *to close*	49
andáre *to go*	1	cíngere *to gird*	71
annéttere *to annex*	122	cógliere *to gather*	10
apparíre *to appear*	33	coincídere *to coincide*	42
appartenére *to belong*	18	concérnere *to concern*	159
appéndere *to hang*	56	conquídere *to conquer*	40
appórre *to affix*	14	comméttere *to commit*	106
appréndere *to learn*	57	commuóvere *to move*	26
apríre *to open*	97	comparíre *to appear*	33
árdere *to burn*	65	compiacére *to please*	6
acéndere *to ascend*	59	compiángere *to pity*	68
aspérgere *to sprinkle*	83	compórre *to compose*	14
assalíre *to assail*	16	compréndere *to understand*	57
assídersi *to sit*	44	comprímere *to compress*	128
assístere *to be present*	138b	comprométtere *compromise*	106
assólvere *to absolve*	141	concédere *to concede, grant*	130

concludere *or* conchiudere
    to conclude 51
concorrere *to concur* 103
condolersi *to sympathize* 20
condurre *to lead, drive* 124
configgere *to drive in* 111
confondere *to confound,*
    mix up 63
congiungere *to join* 78
connettere *to connect* 122
conoscere *to know* 135
consistere *to consist* 138b
contendere *to contend* 60
contenere *to contain* 18
contorcere *to twist* 94
contraddire *to contradict* 5
contraffare *to counterfeit* 4
contrarre *to contract* 9
contundere *to bruise* 64
convenire *to agree* 19
convergere *to converge* 90
convincere *to convince* 93
coprire *to cover* 98
correggere *to correct* 118
correre *to run* 103
corrispondere *to correspond* 1
corrompere *to corrupt* 137
costringere *to force* 144
costruire *to construct* 127
crescere *to grow* 134
cuocere *to cook* 25
dare *to give* 2
decidere *to decide* 41
decrescere *to decrease* 134
dedurre *to deduce* 124
deludere *to disappoint* 51
deporre *to depose* 14

deprimere *to depress* 128
deridere *to deride* 43
desumere *to infer* 105
descrivere *to describe* 125
detergere *to clean* 89
devolvere *to devolve* 139
difendere *to defend* 55
diffondere *to diffuse* 63
dimettere *to remove* 106
dipendere *to depend* 56
dipingere *to paint* 73
dire *to say, tell* 5
dirigere *to direct* 107
dirompere *to break* 137
discendere *to descend* 59
dischiudere *to disclose* 49
disciogliere *to untie,*
    dissolve 147
discorrere *to talk* 103
discutere *to discuss* 123
disfare *to undo* 4
disgiungere *to separate* 78
disilludere *to disappoint* 51
disperdere *to disperse* 66
dispiacere *to displease* 6
disporre *to dispose* 14
dissolvere *to dissolve* 141
dissuadere *to dissuade* 34
distendere *to stretch* 60
distinguere *to distinguish* 76
distogliere *to dissuade* 148
distorcere *to distort* 94
distrarre *to distract* 9
distruggere *to destroy* 119
divellere *to uproot* 11
divenire *to become* 19
dividere *to divide* 45

dolere *to ache, hurt*	20	godere *to enjoy*	143
dovere *to have to, must*	31	illudere *to delude, beguile*	51
eccellere *to excel*	96	immergere *to immerse*	84
effondere *to pour out*	63	imporre *to impose*	14
eleggere *to elect*	114	imprimere *to imprint,*	
elidere *to elide*	38	*impress*	128
eludere *to elude*	51	incidere *to cut*	41
emergere *to emerge*	84	includere *to include*	51
emettere *to emit*	106	incorrere *to incur*	103
ergere *to erect*	85	increscere *to be sorry, regret*	134
erigere *to erect*	107	incutere *to strike*	123
erompere *to break*	137	indulgere *to indulge*	91
escludere *to exclude*	51	inurre *to induce*	124
esigere *to exact, require*	109	inferire *to infer*	102
esimersi *to withdraw from*	160	infliggere *to inflict*	110
espellere *to expel*	95	infrangere *to break*	69
esplodere *to explode*	48	infondere *to infuse*	63
esporre *to expose*	14	inserire *to insert*	151
esprimere *to express*	128	insistere *to insist*	138b
estendere *to extend*	60	intendere *to mean, intend*	60
estinguere *to extinguish*	76	intercedere *to intercede*	130
estorcere *to take away, wrest*	94	interdire *to interdict*	5
estrarre *to extract*	9	interporre *to interpose*	14
evadere *to evade*	35	interrompere *to interrupt*	136
fare *to do, make*	4	intervenire *to intervene*	19
fervere *to be hot*	161	intraprendere *to undertake*	57
figgere *to fix*	111	intravedere *to glimpse*	138
fingere *to pretend*	72	intridere *to temper*	46
fondere *to melt*	63	introdurre *to introduce*	124
frammettere *to interpose*	106	intrudere *to intrude*	52
frangere *to break*	69	invadere *to invade*	35
frapporre *to interpose*	14	involgere *to wrap*	92
friggere *to fry*	113	irrompere *to rush upon*	136
fungere *to act as*	77	iscriversi *to enroll*	125
genuflettersi *to genuflect*	121	istruire *to instruct*	127
giacere *to lie*	8	ledere *to hurt, offend*	37
giungere *to arrive*	78	leggere *to read*	114

91

licere *to be permitted* 154
maledire *to curse* 5
manomettre *to tamper with* 106
mantenere *to maintain* 18
mettere *to put* 106
molcere *to soothe* 155
mordere *to bite* 67
morire *to die* 28
muovere *to move* 26
mungere *to milk* 79
nascere *to be born* 131
nascondere *to hide* 62
negligere *to neglect* 115
nuocere *to hurt* 24
occorrere *to be necessary* 103
offendere *to offend* 55
offrire *to offer* 99
omettere *to omit* 106
opporre *to oppose* 14
opprimere *to oppress* 128
ottenere *to obtain* 18
parere *to seem* 32
percorrere *to travel over* 103
percuotere *to strike* 27
perdere *to lose* 66
permettere *to permit* 106
persuadere *to persuade* 34
pervenire *to arrive at* 19
piacere *to please* 6
piangere *to cry* 68
piovere *to rain* 133
porgere *to offer, give* 87
porre *to put* 14
posporre *to postpone* 14
possedere *to own* 17
potere *to be able, may, can* 23
prediligere *to prefer* 116

predire *to predict* 5
prefiggersi *to take into one's head* 112
preludere *to forecast, come before* 51
prendere *to take* 57
preporre *to prefer* 14
prescegliere *to choose from, among* 146
prescrivere *to prescribe* 125
presiedere *to preside* 17
presumere *to presume* 105
pretendere *to pretend* 60
prevalere *to prevail* 15
prevedere *to foresee* 138
prevenire *to anticipate* 19
produrre *to produce* 14
proferire *to utter* 101
profondere *to pour out* 63
promettere *to promise* 106
promuovere *to promote* 26
propendere *to incline* 149
proporre *to propose* 14
prorompere *to burst out* 137
prosciogliere *to free, absolve* 147
procrivere *to proscribe* 125
proteggere *to protect* 117
provenire *to come from* 19
provvedere *to provide* 138
pungere *to sting* 80
racchiudere *to enclose, shut up* 49
raccogliere *to gather* 10
radere *to shave* 36
raggiungere *to reach* 78
rapprendere *to coagulate, thicken* 57

rattenere *to restrain*	18
rattorcere *to wring*	94
ravvedersi *to repent*	138
ravvolgere *to wrap up*	92
recidere *to cut off*	41
redigere *to write*	108
redimere *to redeem*	104
reggere *to support*	119
rendere *to render*	58
reprimere *to repress*	128
rescindere *to rescind*	129
respingere *to push back*	74
restringere *to restrain*	144
retrocedere *to draw back*	130
riammettere *to admit again, readmit*	106
ricadere *to fall again*	136
richiedere *to request*	39
riconoscere *to recognize*	135
ricoprire *to cover again*	98
ricorrere *to have recourse to, apply to*	103
ridere *to laugh*	43
ridire *to say again*	5
ridurre *to reduce*	124
rifare *to do again*	4
riflettere *to reflect*	120
rifrangere *to refract*	69
rifulgere *to shine*	145
rilucere *to shine*	156
rimanere *to remain*	13
rimettere *to put back*	106
rimordere *to bite again, feel remorse*	67
rimpiangere *to regret*	68
rinascere *to be born again*	131
rinchiudere *to shut in*	49
rincrescere *to regret*	134
rinvenire *to find, to recover*	19
ripercuotere *to strike again*	27
riporre *to put again*	14
riprendere *to retake, recover*	57
riprodurre *to reproduce*	124
risapere *to know*	142
riscuotere *to collect, cash*	27
risolvere *to resolve*	141
risorgere *to rise up again*	88
rispondere *to answer, reply*	61
ristringere *to restrain*	144
ritenere *to retain*	18
ritogliere *to recapture, retake*	148
ritrarre *to draw*	9
riuscire *to succeed*	30
rivedere *to see again*	138
rivivere *to live again*	125
rivolgersi *to turn to, to apply to*	92
rodere *to gnaw*	47
rompere *to break*	137
salire *to ascend, climb*	16
sapere *to know*	142
scadere *to expire, to be due*	136
scegliere *to choose*	146
scendere *to descend*	59
schiudere *to disclose*	49
scindere *to separate*	129
sciogliere *to dissolve, melt*	147
scommettere *to bet*	106
scomparire *to disappear*	33
scomporre *to undo*	14
sconfiggere *to defeat*	111
sconnettere *to disconnect*	122
sconvolgere *to overturn*	92
scoprire *to discover*	97

93

scorgere *to perceive* 86
scorrere *to flow* 103
scrivere *to write* 125
scuotere *to shake* 27
sedere *to sit* 17
seppellire *to bury* 140
smettere *to cease* 106
smuovere *to move* 26
socchiudere *to half shut* 49
soccorrere *to assist* 103
soddisfare *to satisfy* 4
soffrire *to suffer* 100
soggiungere *to add* 78
solere *to be accustomed* 21
sommergere *to submerge* 84
sopprimere *to suppress* 128
sorgere *to rise* 88
sorprendere *to surprise* 57
sorreggere *to support* 118
sorridere *to smile* 43
sospendere *to suspend* 56
sospingere *to push* 74
sostenere *to support* 18
sottintendere *to imply* 60
sovvenire *to remember* 19
spandere *to spill, shed* 53
spargere *to spread, scatter* 82
spegnere *to extinguish, switch off* 12
spendere *to spend* 56
sperdersi *to be lost, to go astray* 66
spiacere *to be sorry, displease* 6
spingere *to push* 74
splendere *to shine* 162
sporgere *to lean out* 87
stare *to stay, stand, be* 3

stendere *to stretch out* 60
storcere *to distort, wrest* 94
stringere *to draw close, clasp* 144
struggere *to consume, pine away* 119
succedere *to happen* 130
supporre *to suppose* 14
svellere *to root out* 11
svenire *to faint away* 19
svolgersi *to take place* 92
tacere *to keep silent* 7
tendere *to tend, hold out* 60
tenere *to hold, have* 18
tergere *to clean, wipe* 89
tingere *to dye* 75
togliere *to take from* 148
torcere *to twist* 94
tradurre *to translate* 124
trafiggere *to run through* 111
transigere *to compromise, come to terms* 109
trarre *to draw, pull* 9
trascorre *to spend (time)* 103
transcrivere *to transcribe* 125
transmettere *to transmit* 106
transparire *to show forth* 33
trattenere *to hold back, detain* 18
travedere *to see wrongly* 138
uccidere *to kill* 42
udire *to hear* 29
ungere *to grease* 81
uscire *to go out* 30
urgere *to be urgent* 157
valere *to be worth* 15
vedere *to see* 138
venire *to come* 19
vigere *to be in force* 158

vilipęndere *to despise*   56 | volęre *to will*   22
vįncere *to win*   93 | vǫlgere *to turn*   92
vįvere *to live*   125

A model English verb

The following is a model of the principal tenses of an English verb. The names of the tenses are those which are generally used in the conjugation of foreign verbs. It is very important to know what English words are represented by the names *present, imperfect, future,* etc. For example, *I am calling* is just as much present as *I call,* and *I shall be calling* and *I shall call* are both future. There's no need to differentiate between the English simple present and present continuous, present perfect and simple past, and all the other variations that appear in English grammar books. But do take special notice of the auxiliaries used in the conjugation of English future and conditional.

INFINITIVE: to call

PRESENT PARTICIPLE: calling

PAST PARTICIPLE: called

PRESENT TENSE:
I call *or* I am calling
you call *or* you are calling (*singular*)
he calls *or* he is calling
we call *or* we are calling
you call *or* you are calling (*plural*)
they call *or* they are calling

IMPERFECT or PAST:
I called *or* I was calling
you called *or* you were calling
he called *or* he was calling

we called *or* we were calling
you called *or* you were calling
they called *or* they were calling

FUTURE:
I shall call *or* I shall be calling
you will call *or* you will be calling
he will call *or* he will be calling
we shall call *or* we shall be calling
you will call *or* you will be calling
they will call *or* they will be calling

CONDITIONAL:
I should call *or* I should be calling
you would call *or* you would be calling
he would call *or* he would be calling
we shall call *or* we should be calling
you would call *or* you would be calling
they would call *or* they would be calling

PERFECT:
I have called *or* I have been calling
you have called *or* you have been calling
he has called *or* he has been calling
we have called *or* we have been calling
you have called *or* you have been calling
they have called *or* they have been calling

PLUPERFECT:
I had called *or* I had been calling, etc.

FUTURE PERFECT:
I shall have called *or* I shall have been calling, etc.

CONDITIONAL PERFECT:
I should have called *or* I should have been calling, etc.

IMPERATIVE: call (you); let/him/us/them call